Women, Wisdom & Dreams

THE LIGHT OF THE FEMININE SOUL

by ANNE SCOTT

NICASIO PRESS
FREESTONE, CALIFORNIA

Women, Wisdom & Dreams

THE LIGHT OF THE FEMININE SOUL

First published in the United States by
Nicasio Press, 2008, in Freestone, California
www.nicasiopress.com

All inquiries should be addressed to:
Anne Scott
DreamWeather Foundation
P.O. Box 2002, Sebastopol, CA 95473

www.dreamweather.org

Cover and book design by Patty Holden

Scott, Anne
Women, Wisdom and Dreams: The light of the feminine soul

Printed in the United States of America

ISBN 978-0-9818636-1-0

I CAN SEE AS CLEAR AS
DAYLIGHT THAT THE
HOUR IS COMING WHEN
WOMEN WILL LEAD HUMANITY
TO A HIGHER EVOLUTION.

———

Hazrat Inayat Khan,
20th century Sufi mystic

FOREWORD

I met Anne Scott in the ways of women, our lives intersecting at various points in the small town where we live. A mutual friend introduced us, and her visit to my dance studio inspired *WomenSpeak*, a series of talks by women (of which she was one); her daughter took my teen dance class, and later we found ourselves at a Women in Business meeting together.

Over time I came to understand more deeply Anne's work with women. Her book, *Serving Fire*, provided nourishment and support for my heartfelt yearning to bring forth the sacredness of family life. I began to participate in her women's circles, which included the silent meditation and the dreamwork that Anne so eloquently puts forth in this book. These gatherings fulfilled my equally deep yearning to come together with women in true intimacy, that all the morning coffee groups, book clubs, mothers' clubs and ladies luncheons could not satisfy.

Anne expanded these gatherings of women to include longer retreats here in the San Francisco Bay Area and then across the United States. I had the great joy to attend many of these, and the privilege to support

Anne in holding the space at some of these events. Concurrently my Zen teacher was encouraging me to help create Rinzai women's Zen practice, and I was co-leading women's retreats in the more formal Zen structure.

This work with women is what truly speaks to my heart now. Like many of those whose dreams appear here in this book, I too have received dreams that have clarified and deepened my connection to the wisdom that resides in all of us, accessible to us if we can release ourselves from compulsive activity and the overwhelming distractions of our culture. And, I would add for women, regaining a sense of self-trust will help us to manifest this deep wisdom.

I recently came across the second volume of the work of Masaru Emoto, who first became known for his work photographing water crystals in their response to verbal communications. I was so struck by the water crystal's response to the word 'confidence,' which is the Japanese equivalent to self-trust. The crystal was beautifully formed, radiantly clear, and emanated a feeling of great strength. That image became a source of deep contemplation for me during a recent retreat.

I would like to offer a vision that came to me during one of Anne's gatherings of women in Taos, New

Mexico. I find myself receiving visions during meditation, sitting or walking in nature, or sometimes just doing the dishes. They feel like a communication or response from some archetypal realm to a deep question that I may or may not have access to consciously. As we were sitting in silence at the end of our three-day retreat, I had the impression I was given a message from the grandmothers—native indigenous women—that came in several parts.

In the first, I was told that women must heal each other. The picture I saw was of a small group of women holding, rocking, and singing to a woman in need of healing. Anne describes so beautifully the metaphoric 'holding in arms' that a circle of women can do for a member going through pain and difficult emotions, through our deep silence and attention. In the second part I understood that women must use their ways of communication. The picture I was given was of an intersecting web of light, where energy traveled very fast from one point to another. Though perhaps this is a picture of the technological worldwide web, women know of a more timeless web of energy that connects us all. And the last part conveyed the message that women must sweat together, the picture being of women hoeing in the fields together. I believe Anne speaks to this mingling of our perspiration and tears in these circles of hope in service to life.

May this book's gathering of feminine wisdom inspire you and ignite a flame in your heart.

—MYOSHO VIRGINIA MATTHEWS
Sebastopol, California
September 24, 2008

CONTENTS

INTRODUCTION

During a difficult time of my life, I had only my dreams to guide me. As I began to understand them, I saw how the shift in consciousness that the dreams brought me became reflected in changes in the circumstances of my life. These personal dreams were followed by more universal dreams, showing me how women can give birth to a sacred quality of being that heals and transforms their lives.

DREAM

I am told that war is everywhere. And, that an antidote is found within women. I then see a vibrant, healing green stream that runs through women from head to toe. I am told that women need to find this stream and recognize it in themselves, so that it can flow out into life.

From these dreams and from my own life and work, I came to realize the power that lies hidden in women, a power that is often released when an experience such as a dream, a loss, or a shock, opens a woman to a new dimension of consciousness. If heeded and tended to with love, this opening awakens her feminine nature.

The work I have done for 20 years has allowed me to listen to women's dreams while conducting retreats, women's circles and gatherings, and collaborating with women from diverse spiritual and religious traditions. Over time, this work has been tested in the field of women's lives. But it wasn't until I had worked with women who had lived through the wrath of Hurricane Katrina, that I realized that this model of healing and change was effective even in the midst of devastation.

I was scheduled to give a retreat to a group of women in Baton Rouge a few days after Hurricane Katrina. I thought the retreat was going to be canceled, but I was asked to come anyway. I stood in the room there feeling somewhat helpless in the face of the catastrophic conditions this group of women, some from New Orleans, now faced. What could I offer to them?

I realized that I could share the dreams that I had gathered from women around the world. These dreams offered potent images that speak of a deeper reality connecting women as one. At the end of the day when the women were asked what they received from our time together, a response of hope echoed around the room.

A year later, when I returned to Baton Rouge to give another retreat, a woman spoke about her experience as a lactation nurse when Hurricane Katrina hit Louisiana. Towards the end of the retreat, after listening to the dreams of other women, a new clarity broke through the beliefs that had confined her life.

"I was in the women's hospital during Katrina. Overhead I could hear the sound of helicopters transporting babies from a hospital in New Orleans. The hospital was darkened due to limited electricity, and I was in a small dimly lit room with a mom and her newborn. On the other side of the room the father was asleep on a cot. I was teaching this young woman how to nurse her baby, when I heard an inner voice that said, '*This* is what it's all about.' All that mattered was to be aware of the sacredness of that moment, although I didn't realize its meaning until today. I can now see how the separate fragments of my life—relationships past and present—are all connected."

From my experiences in Baton Rouge, I decided to write this book to make the dreams of women available to many other women, and to provide tools for understanding the language of dreams. For we must each offer our deepest attention to the glimmers and whispers of new life that beckon to us—whether our own, or those we see and hear in our communities.

We are each so valuable in this infinitely greater scheme of things. Our dreams and stories speak of what is coming alive and awakening during this time of great uncertainty.

This book is intended to help women, and men, access and make conscious their forgotten or hidden wisdom and their potential for self-healing. This is vital work. For when we heal ourselves, we heal and nourish life. Reclaiming the language of dreams, cultivating states of awareness and stillness in our lives, and gathering in groups to share from a deeper place, offer rich ways to reconnect to the joy, love, and creativity that are our birthright and our contribution to life.

—ANNE SCOTT

PART ONE

DREAMWORK

Learning the Language of the Soul

What if you slept, and what if in your sleep

you dreamed, and what if in your dream you went

to heaven and there plucked a strange and

beautiful flower, and what if when you awoke you

had the flower in your hand. Ah, what then?

—SAMUEL TAYLOR COLERIDGE

WHY WE NEED TO
LISTEN TO OUR DREAMS

Our modern culture has lost its understanding of the inner world. As a result the unconscious has become something to be feared rather than a fertile garden. We forget that at night, when we close the door to our daily activities, we can rest in the infinite and be nourished by our dreams. Instead, many of us lie awake, worry or wonder about the next day, or the next problem, instead of resting in the creative abode of silence.

Dreams and meditation are valuable tools to help us create a bridge to the unconscious, to access our own innate wisdom. Dreams, in particular, help us touch the wellspring, the creative spark of knowing, which is a gift from the divine. Each dream, like a poem, is a kernel from the inner world. The simple turning of our attention inward, and learning to value our dreams, can help us heal what has separated us from our wholeness.

DREAMS AS GUIDANCE

Dreams are a precious doorway through which the energy from the inner world can be made conscious, ultimately guiding us towards healing our wounds and reviving life. Dreams provide hints to find such healing. And because we are all different, for each of us this process is uniquely our own.

To receive the wisdom of dreams, it is not necessary to delve into the unconscious. The messages emerge as they will. We can learn to hold a space in which our rational mind does not interfere, where the deepest part of our self is held sacred and can speak to us.

DREAMS GIVE VOICE
TO OUR LONGING

A woman carries the wholeness of life within her, even if she isn't aware of it. When she begins to look within, a deep longing arises which may not be understood. This longing to reconnect with our wholeness is the root of life, the root of our existence. If the roots of a tree are cut, the tree will wither and die from lack of water. Sadly, this has been the effect of our Western culture. For centuries we have valued the rational world and denied the inner world of the feminine. We have learned to see everything as separate, thereby cutting ourselves off from the flow of grace from inner to outer. For this we are crying in our depths.

Many women experience this longing and think it is a problem, one of depression, isolation and loneliness. We don't realize it is a call from another place, a call for help, maybe a *cry* for help. We may try to fill the emptiness we feel with more activity, or with food, relationships, drugs or alcohol, without learning about life itself. This understanding is not reflected in our culture. But dreams and meditation can reconcile this separation. When we realize that life needs our attention, we can listen to what it is asking of us.

———

DREAM

I see an ancient bird in the sky. It is so unsightly that I am repelled by its appearance. Then it falls to the ground and when it touches the earth, it turns into a woman. She is emaciated, with barely any skin on her bones, and I cannot even look at her for more than a second. But a voice tells me that I have to take her in and care for her, and that after a year this woman will be healed. Then she will work with me and care for my house.

THE BIRD IS AN ANCIENT SYMBOL for the soul, or consciousness. The earth is the ground from which we create our lives. If a bird appears in a dream as hungry, or dying, we know that somehow we have lost our way and need to align with the deeper needs of our soul. This dream suggests that with a willingness to face her 'wounding' and bring it down to earth with compassion, the dreamer can heal her soul, her feminine nature, and be able to join with and nourish life.

A DREAM DOES NOT NECESSARILY HAVE TO BE UNDERSTOOD

Dreams show us what we need to know, over time. If a woman accepts a dream as the beginning of a fertile process, and learns simply to hold it with curiosity and acceptance, then this vital energy, this forgotten language, can begin to tell the truth of who she is.

DREAM

I have had a recurring dream for years. I am in a city and don't know where to go or how to reach my destination. I am lost. I can't find my car, keys, or purse. After I became aware of its meaning, I had another dream. This time, instead of being lost, I was found.

JUST LIKE A POEM, a dream carries within it its own wisdom. If a woman can hold a dream's energy without trying to logically or rationally understand it, the meaning will unfold. This doesn't mean that the dream's hidden symbols are ignored, since every individual has her own relationship with the images that come from within. While some symbols are universal, there is no textbook explanation for our dream images; the unique message of a dream needs to be allowed in. For instance, for one woman, a ring may represent a family heirloom, and for another, her own marriage, or her own wholeness.

AT DIFFICULT TIMES DREAMS
ARISE, SHIFT AND CHANGE

The spirit of our dream life is like the natural world that moves, changes and fluctuates according to the seasons and cycles of nature. When we ignore the forces of nature, we become cut off from this potent aspect of life. During times of difficulty, however, dreams burst through our complacency, trying to reconnect us with what is essential and showing us a different way of living from our wholeness.

When I was first learning to work with and value dreams, my dreams came as messengers, to heal and guide me.

———

DREAM

I am shown a circle with a dot in the center, and am told that this dot is love. And, if I can be this love, the problems in my family will fall away.
I am suddenly inside the dot in the center of the circle. Waves upon waves pour through my entire body, filling me with love.

I LEARNED TO HOLD the energy of love, rather than dissipating it by focusing on my problems. It became a daily practice, while cooking, walking, or driving to town. I now knew that a love like this existed, whether or not I could feel it in the midst of difficulties. When I reverted to dwelling on my difficulties, a dream would come to turn my attention again towards love. When one can catch hold of the feeling of love in a dream, it becomes easier during the day to live from this transforming source.

DREAMS CAN INITIATE US
INTO NATURAL WAYS OF BEING

Our real nature nourishes and is nourished by life. Sometimes we can discover our natural way of being through our dreams, which can show us how to live more closely attuned with the divine qualities of our soul.

DREAM

I'm standing at the ocean, talking with a friend.
There are two opalescent lights, one in the
crashing ocean waves, the other, which I realize
is a feather, on the ground. I jump down to see it
but it becomes a mother eagle, and I am suddenly
in her nest! She grabs hold of my right arm with
her feet and squeezes it tightly. I feel the strength
and warmth of her talons. I know not to resist as
she could kill me. I relax.

THE RIGHT ARM CAN SIGNIFY the work one does in the world. The dreamer knows from an earlier dream that her purpose is to create beauty. She lives this purpose through her work as a jeweler. Yet this work stems from a place of such vulnerability that she often doubts its value. This is how our logical consciousness can cover up our natural way of being.

The eagle is considered to be the only bird that can look directly at the sun. As happened for the dreamer, this illuminated aspect of our nature can grab hold of us, and refuse to let us go, even when we run away from ourselves. An eagle is a potent symbol, requiring the dreamer to become conscious of its association with the earth and her own soul. What was most important to the dreamer was the feeling of the powerful eagle's grip on her arm. She knew that she could now begin to claim this inner strength.

A CONSTRICTING OR DESTRUCTIVE internalized pattern can be healed through conscious awareness and unconditional love, and it is often our dreams that will first reveal these patterns to us. One woman dreamt that she kept her treasured pearl necklace hidden deep in her pocket so that no one would notice it. Another woman had a dream of a man taking all of her belongings. When he tries to steal the beautiful necklace that her grandfather had given to her, she refuses to give it away.

It takes great strength to witness our inner patterns, to pray and to hold them in our heart where they can be healed. An illustration of this comes to mind when I think of times I have felt excluded from people, events, or life itself. It is an old and deceptive pattern that can appear in my dreams, and which remains with me the next day. I can take a long walk, acutely aware of this pain, and place it in my heart. Almost imperceptibly, I will begin to notice the wind, the twist of the limbs of an old oak tree, the creek filled with last night's rain. A sense of participation and communion with life returns, and I am no longer separate from creation.

Dreams too can change quickly with this kind of love and attention. Once the shift happens, the natural nobility of the masculine aspect can help a woman to live her soul's truth.

For the dreamer of the 'ocean' dream above, how would it look if she truly lived the way of the eagle? The eagle is fierce, unwilling to let the dreamer diminish her life or creative work. The eagle's grip is a security, a comfort to the dreamer, and gives her an inner dignity. If the dreamer can own this quality, then her jewelry making will help her to live her wholeness in the world.

DREAM

I am in an empty house when I see hundreds of hummingbirds outside the window, flying together, forming a single, living force. I don't know if I should let them in.

WE ARE OFTENTIMES unfamiliar with the power of our natural force, free of cultural constrictions and conditioned fears. On occasion a dream will reveal a woman's fear of violation as this life force awakens, as a love tries to burst forth from within. Many women have known violation from outside of themselves. But this love is different. It comes from the inside, pushing through our conditioning, opening us to the wholeness of our deepest nature.

DREAMS HELP US
TO CHOOSE LIFE

Many of us find ways to avoid life, whether we know it or not. We might hold back instinctively, because of old fears or wounds. We might busy ourselves with multiple activities that distract us from pain or vulnerability, but which prevent us from joining with life at a deeper level. Or we might even use a spiritual path as an excuse to keep us from actively engaging with 'ordinary' life.

DREAM

A man tells me, "Life flows through women. In order to allow life to come through, a woman must choose life. Otherwise the collective culture will shut life down."

THE DREAMER EXPLAINED, "Somehow I have a picture that in order to be of service to life I have to be doing some *Big* thing, helping lots of people or whatever. And yet it's not that way at all. Devotion to the experience of life is different. Choosing again and again

Life. Sometimes this can be so deeply challenged by the unknown, or by poverty or illness, or loss. Yet the living of it, the devotion to it, is a choice every day. I will consciously choose life even if it means only one small part of me can stay open in the moment."

DREAM

I see a pregnant woman who is having a sonogram. A friend holds up the sonogram image for me to look at and explains, "Here, at the umbilical cord, is the place in a woman where the personal connects with the universal."

THE INSIGHT REVEALED to the dreamer was that she could respect her own need for sustenance from a gathering of indigenous women elders that she had wanted to attend. Previously, she had ignored her feelings and decided it wasn't essential. Yet the dream showed her that her personal longing was linked to a universal need for nourishment of the feminine.

Life asks that instead of keeping the intimacy of our inner life sealed off from what we do, we learn to truly live, and allow our love for the sacred, which is a power in and of itself.

DREAMS GIVE ACCESS
TO THE FEMININE SOUL

When did a collective shame over the rejected feminine soul take root? This has taken place so gradually, over centuries, that we don't quite realize the devastating effect this separation has had on our perception of women, the receptive aspect of life, or the earth. But we must now relearn this lost language of the soul, as our full consciousness is vitally needed to bring new life at a time such as ours, when the old structures are falling away.

Every young girl somewhere knows wholeness, the state of union with her soul. She may not call it God or the sacred, but when she looks outside at night and sees a star, in that moment she has touched her own essence, and felt connected to all of life and the spirit within. That moment comes as grace. Too often this magic is forgotten.

Yet our dreams give us access to the forgotten wisdom that we need for our lives and for life itself. Once we turn our attention to them, we learn to adjust to their cycles, the way dreams come and go like the seasons. Sometimes we hunger for their nourishment, for that reconnection to the inner world, but at other times they seem to leave us alone in our outer life. At times, after confusing dreams, it can seem that we have lost a connection altogether. But with faith in our deeper wisdom, a dream will eventually come, a dream filled with simplicity and clarity. We begin to trust the process of allowing dreams to unfold in their own time, with their own rhythms.

THE WISDOM OF DREAMS
LIES BEYOND THE MIND

There is a level of relating to dreams that is rarely known in the West. This is the place in which we respect a deeper wisdom, without which we cannot drink from the wellspring of our dream.

A woman dreamt that she was in her bedroom and heard someone knocking softly three times on the door. This was a recurring dream that brought up her fear of violation. She sent her dream to an online dream analyst. The 'dream expert' told her that it was just an anxiety dream with no importance. He assuaged her fears and told her basically to forget about it. A logical, possibly helpful response. But where is the mystery of the soul? Where is her own deepest longing?

In the intimacy of the bedroom, where we sleep, where we love, an unknown figure knocks softly at the door of her heart. This knocking calls her attention to the depth within herself, that soft, listening place. When something is repeated three times in a dream, it usually signifies sacred importance, calling us to go beyond our habitual response to reject what lies beyond the mind.

How different it would be for the dreamer, if she knew that she could welcome her own Self!

I once met a woman who had been to many workshops, until one day she had a warning dream.

I am at a workshop sitting in a circle with other women. The workshop leader stands in the middle of the room holding a beautiful woman's necklace of beads in his hands. He takes the beads apart, one by one, to show us what is inside the necklace, but the necklace crumbles into dust and falls to the ground.

A NECKLACE IS A WOMAN'S TRUE WAY of being in the world. We each have been raised with a certain conditioning that may have been helpful at one point, but later becomes restrictive and confining. As a woman becomes aware of her need to live in connection to her deepest self, dreams can come from the interior of her feminine soul, a distant landscape where her childhood or cultural conditioning cannot reach.

This dream describes the mystery that turns to dust if we approach it solely with rational consciousness. Instead, we learn to care for our dreams as we would nurture a seed. A dream is a living energy. We can learn to hold it as something sacred. This means knowing if it can be shared with a friend, or if it needs to remain in the silence of your heart, where its meaning will unfold over time. Sometimes, a dream may not be fully understood for years.

Dreams are messengers bearing images that heal and restore life. We need to be attentive to them. We don't need to *do* anything with a dream. We simply hold the dream lightly, aware of it but without trying to analyze it. You can feel your way with a dream, and be aware of what it evokes in you. You could discover that a dream is not personal. It may be an understanding or an insight for you to simply witness.

THE POWER OF DREAMS

A former college teacher had never worked with her dreams, had never even listened to them. She came to the women's group I led for years in my studio on the hill by our house. The joy of her soul was restored as she learned the meaning and language of her inner life. In her words:

"At first I didn't pay attention because everyone says, 'It's just a dream,' but then I learned to value them. Over the years, just listening to the dreams has made me value life in a whole new way—more deeply, more respectfully. Life becomes precious. I don't think I could be with so many people in my current work if it weren't for my dreams. They have changed me, they made me whole.

"There was a period in which I had dreams that were more like experiences," she says. "They repeated themselves until I was able to witness with a compassionate neutrality. The teaching was in the repetition.

"I was told that I had to watch a scene without flinching. Even a blink, and I would have to witness it again. I had to witness the tragic enormity of certain things, until I could be present without a thought. I had to watch the death of my mother, my beloved cat, and the collapse of the twin towers. And then they became a part of my physical heart. My cat stopped coming to me in dreams, begging, because he is here in my heart, an inseparable part of me. And what this makes me *do*," she said quietly, "*is just love*."

"I learned that I had to write my dreams down. If I didn't, they would pass by like a stone skipping along the surface of water; I would have forgotten them. Then the dreams worked on me. I didn't always want to do it, but they took the unbearable, the unthinkable, and turned it into a root of compassion that I felt in my body. This is the power of a dream."

DREAMWORK PRACTICES

I t is a good practice to write down your dreams regularly in the morning, or during the night if you awaken from a dream. This sends a message that you are receptive, that you are listening, and will often make it easier for you to recall your dreams. This is how to welcome the wisdom that comes from our depths.

Writing down a dream gives permission to accept this source of wisdom. Once a dream is written down, it is preserved. And then we must give our dreams time to reveal their meaning.

When we have a dream which brings us a sense of peace, intimacy, or strength, we need to be aware that this quality is for healing. We learn to respect our dreams and the deep place they come from. This is the mystery we need to hold in mind. A dream is not for our personal gain but to help us heal, and to live our creative potential.

Write freely, as the details and the feelings come to you. Allow the dream to speak its truth, without embellishing or trying to make it more interesting. Include the

whole dream, even the parts you don't think are signifi-
cant. These rejected parts often have great meaning.

When reflecting upon a dream, consider the different characters in the dream as parts of yourself. For
instance, dreaming of one's husband is not necessarily
a literal dream about him, but about some masculine
aspect of oneself. What is more important is to consider
what a certain dream character means to you. You will
then see a part of yourself being brought to your attention by the dream.

Our dreams speak to us in symbols, in images which
evoke feelings or associations. We learn to work with
these symbols, holding them, allowing them to speak in
their own way. Since dreams are fluid and not fixed, they
will change over time with your conscious awareness.
Your task is not to interpret and understand; this will
come naturally. What is more important is to hold your
dreams with attention and love.

If a dream brings sorrow, fear, or longing, hold this
feeling in your heart. Our heart has an infinite capacity
to embrace difficult feelings, and to transform them.

There are times when we cannot write down a
dream. We know when such a dream comes, for we want

only to hold it in silence. Like any new relationship, we each find our own way with our dreams. It is a way that we learn to relate to our hidden wisdom.

SAMPLE DREAMWORK PROCESS

One woman had a powerful dream after she returned from a vacation to India. She eventually forgot the dream. Six months later she came to a retreat that I led. The night before the retreat she remembered this dream:

> I was in India. A woman was showing me a baby elephant. This woman had neutered the mother elephant, and took the elephant baby home with her to America. She gave it to me and I held the baby elephant in my arms, but I didn't know how to feed it and felt the anguish of not caring for it.

WHEN THE DREAMER told this dream, she experienced the grief that she felt for the baby elephant. She wanted to nourish it, and felt the pain of having rejected it. All these months had passed since the dream came to her, yet still it carried the power to touch her with its significance.

The elephant is a symbol of her Self. This is her wholeness, her soul or essence which was touched by her visit in India. We do not know how to care for this part of ourselves that is the core of our being. In our rushing around we cover it over, and a dream like this can recede back into the unconscious, an opportunity lost.

The Self is expressed through different images, and the elephant is one of them. Other symbols are a flower, a diamond, the Christ, Buddha, a swan, an ancient stone, or a golden child. It is the feeling of an image that helps us touch a dream, and we in turn are intimately touched by the dream's power to bring change to our life. In this case, the dreamer will need to discover what the dream means for her, and to care for this deeper part of her being.

After all these months, her dream had come alive again. Such is the dream's miracle. A dream waits, sometimes for years, until we are ready to receive its potent meaning. If she can hold this dream in her conscious awareness and not forget it, she will learn how to nourish the birth of a new consciousness, which will help her to live more closely attuned to her soul.

QUESTIONS AND ANSWERS
ABOUT DREAMWORK

Q: *I have learned the importance of dreams, and the messages in dreams, but I'm at a loss as to how to work with my own dreams. Can you explain how I can work with this dream?*

There is a naked little baby—not old enough to turn over on its own, not more than three months, and I think she is female. I place the baby in a zippered plastic storage bag, the kind that a comforter or bedding comes in. I cushion the baby among some sweaters, colored mostly red. When I zipper it shut, I leave an opening for air so the baby can breathe, and then place the container under my bed for storage, like you would store your winter clothes in the spring season.

I woke up feeling that this was important. I feel that I'm placing in storage what is in my heart, cushioned among my favorite red sweaters, until I have time to nurture my baby and let her grow. But I made sure she had air to breathe, so she is with me, waiting....

A: I wonder if there is a different way to allow this baby to become part of your life now. The red color of the sweaters indicates the need for life, but I'm not so sure that a baby will survive in a plastic bag with just enough air to breathe. I know it's logical to keep her under your bed until spring, but she's not a sweater, she is a newborn baby.

Maybe you can take her out of the plastic bag and give her some milk. This baby does not live in time, so you can nourish her without having to spend time with her. It has to do with responding to her needs. This is about oneness. It pushes against our ideas and beliefs, and says there is a different way, wanting to be born. I'm sure that if you returned to your dream and took your baby out of the bag, then she would be much happier, and so would you. She won't have to take up your time. What she needs is to be loved, and to be given a space in your life.

Q: *How does one go into a dream as you suggest, and work with it, nurture it, etc.? I know I'm speaking from my practical, logical, solution-focused mind, but I'm asking for some guidance as to how one goes about doing this.*

A: There is a quality of *allowing* in this way of working. One just allows oneself to *be* with a dream. Nothing needs to happen, really. It is a deeply feminine way of working. These 'babies' don't need much. But they do need our awareness and receptivity.

Imagine that it is something like seeing a real baby, and holding her in your arms. It has more to do with finding your way to this place inside of you, perhaps when you take a walk or in the moments before you go to sleep. Just hold the baby in your attention. And then you do what you would naturally do if you were with a baby. It would be hard to hold her in a zippered bag, so perhaps you could hold her more closely, in your heart. Maybe you will only be able to remember for a few seconds here or there. It's not that you have to do this daily, but it is more a way of attending to something from time to time, just as we wouldn't leave a pot of soup cooking on the stove untended for too long. This is a woman's way of working with life.

PART TWO

GATHERING TOGETHER

Imagine columns of light that reach from earth

to heaven. That is who we are. We need only

come together from our different communities,

and in the space between our differences

oneness can nourish the earth.

THE SPIRIT OF CHANGE

There is a value and strong need for individuals and groups to come together now, to witness and practice the healing work which transforms not only those of us who commune for the sake of the inner life, but which transforms the collective as well. This is how women have worked in ancient times. Today, we can remember in a new way the significance of restoring the link between feminine spirituality and social change.

When we come together without judgment, creating a sacred space for the truth in each of us, love pours through our differences and unites us. We become the vehicles for an awakening which can take place in our own lives. There is a beauty to this that is unrelated to our problems. Within it are the qualities of peace, healing, and nourishment for life.

My work listening to the dreams of women in different parts of the country and around the world has made clear to me that women need to sit in circles. When we gather together, sharing our dreams, the stories from our lives, and the silence, we are each touched and nourished from within. We make a space for the soul.

I began to work with groups of women in this way many years ago. A teacher of mine told me simply, "Learn to hold something and nothing at the same time." I had to learn to create a space, and not impose anything on the group, but to listen, and to want nothing for myself. This way of being was initially frightening, mostly because it was unfamiliar. I had the following dream at this time:

> *I am preparing for a women's group when a great wind blows through my house. It's so terrifying that I jump into bed and pull the covers over me. My husband says, "You need to stand up or else the wind will destroy you."*

WHAT IS THE WIND but the spirit of change, of healing, which serves the soul—which serves life? I had to learn, through mistakes, when I was trying to *do* something in a group, and learn simply to be present, attentive, and to listen. My dreams helped me align with this feminine way. Most of all, I found it required trust, and this can only come with time and experience. This can be difficult for women who have been hurt, and who have created patterns of protection. There is an old Sufi prayer: *Please empty myself of all except Thy presence.* This is the feminine way of being—receptive, open, alive with our natural devotion.

A WOMAN FROM GERMANY had a dream that helped to deepen my understanding of this practice of being:

> *A wise old woman tells me, "When enough come together, the world will change. This must be done in the way of women."*

It has been valuable for me to work with women of diverse cultural and spiritual traditions, because I have seen how the energy of love flows through our differences. We need these differences. Leading groups with women friends such as a Zen Buddhist lay-ordained nun, a community leader from Mexico with Catholic and Aztec heritage, a Sufi with Pakistani and British background, an Episcopal priest in Georgia, and a Blackfoot environmental scientist from Canada, I have seen that while our paths are different, what we have in common supports us in strengthening and giving confidence to women to live from their true self.

Each woman stands in the center of her own life stream. Once we know our true value, we are not so quick to judge ourselves or others, or to see ourselves through comparisons. In a group, the open-hearted sharing heals our fragmentation or isolation. This work of both attending to each other and to the silence, with heart and presence, builds a bridge to the greater Circle of which we are all a part.

Carl Jung wrote that when women are restored to wholeness, generations before them and after them also are healed. All unnecessary obstacles are cleared out of the way of the life-stream that is meant to flow through us.

STARTING A CIRCLE

When I was talking with a group in Alabama, a woman asked me, "How can women come together for the greater good, and learn to trust each other?"

This is what we are learning to do as we meet together. A deep trust forms when our intention is to be in service to life.

To start a group gathering, you need only two or more women. It is best to set a regular rhythm for the gatherings, perhaps two to three hours, once or twice a month. No preparation is required, just the sincere desire to be of service to the women in your community. Here are some guidelines you can adapt in your own way:

- Every woman is accepted, just as she is. No one is judged. Each woman is valued equally. This is a nonhierarchical way of being together, although one woman may hold the group, in the sense that it may be her home, or her initial idea.

- This group is based upon individuals, each with her own unique connection to the divine—the essence that resides in each of us. A group of women oriented in this way can work together as an organic network of souls. The water of life can nourish them simply through being together.

- Meditate in silence. Silence is universal, and brings a sense of calm and clarity.

- Open the space for women to share their dreams, or perhaps to speak about their inner lives. Often, when a dream or experience is shared aloud, the dreamer will understand her dream in a new way. We can help each other by offering our own intuition or thoughts about a dream. But ultimately, the only one who can truly understand her dream is the woman herself.

MEDITATION PRACTICE

When women come together, as a group of unique individuals with common intent and open hearts, it is good to begin with a form of silent meditation, either of the heart, or whatever form of silence women choose. The silence holds and heals. Through our hearts, life is nourished.

Meditation is a powerful way to begin a gathering. It honors every individual's faith, and allows us to be together in the universal feminine container of love. Finding our own way of silence, in which we can be with our deepest self, gives us strength and, above all, connects us to the divine feminine.

GROUP DREAMWORK

When a dream is shared in a group, simply listening is the first step. The feminine way of listening is the most healing way to welcome the dream into life. This means that we create a space, which is essentially a container woven out of the threads of our awareness, our attention, and love. This creates a way to hold a dream, to listen to it without imposing our own ideas onto its meaning.

Then, it is always important to ask the dreamer what is the feeling of her dream. This leads the way to the life-stream flowing beneath the storyline. As the dream's feeling content is explored, the dreamer often comes to a new understanding of the dream that hadn't occurred to her.

This simple practice of listening to the soul, with other women, can change your life. It will speak to you from your own wisdom, opening you to your own devotion and love for life. And, the healing work that we do in this way, listening to each others' dreams and experiences, meditating together, ripples out far beyond our own personal lives, touching life itself. We are interconnected, part of all life.

DREAM

I am recently retired. I have wanted to know what
my purpose is, and what to do with my life. I've
had many recurring dreams of dark, empty houses.
This has gone on for months. But after I recently
told the dream to a friend, something changed.
My next house dream is filled with the activity
of several generations of women. I tell the elder
women that I am cleaning up after them. I am
pulling up all the dead plants around the house,
pulling them up by their roots.

SHARING HER DREAM with me as I listened deeply,
helped take this dream to the next level for the dreamer.
She realized that she had been neglecting her inner life.
Her recurring dream of dark, empty houses had been
persistently knocking at her door for years. It wasn't
until she shared it that she became conscious of its
meaning, and began to understand how it revealed her
deeper purpose. To have just a glimpse of this purpose
was enough to restore in her a sense of wonder.

THE POWER OF WITNESSING

Sometimes deep feeling will arise for a woman in the process of sharing or contemplating a dream. If we can learn to witness, and to listen from our heart, rather than trying to console or comfort, then healing can take place at the very core of a woman's being.

A young woman once told a dream that revealed a deep wounding of the feminine and of violation. She began to weep quietly. No one interfered as an intense silence filled the room. It grew until it could hold the depths of her ancient pain that no longer seemed only personal, but universal. Her crying slowly subsided, leaving in its wake a vast and dynamic sense of peace. No words were needed. Soon after, this young woman got married and had a child. It was as if the pain that she carried had been released and transformed. The life stream could now flow through her.

As we heal, love enters into the dark places in a woman's body, and also into the earth. When one woman heals, it becomes easier for other women in the collective to access their own source of healing.

DREAM

I am walking around a city square that is surrounded by a large body of water. I am being stalked by two men. I turn towards the middle of the square. Next I am with two women at the edge of the water. I begin telling this dream; it just comes out. I tell the rest of it and how I was caught and raped after walking in the square. When I am finished telling, I go silent and silence is everywhere. In a way I am hearing it for the first time. There seems to be a space in me that is in need of less reaction. I just wait, still. It is almost as if the telling, the confessing, is an echo of what is inside other women. We tell, we hear, and we know inside. It is as if this simple act is necessary for healing.

PART THREE

RESTORING STILLNESS
TO OUR LIVES

DREAM

I am told that silence is my church.

CREATING SPACE

Through our dreams, when our conditioned mind is at rest, we are able to contact the deeper knowing of the feminine and hold it in trust. We also need to learn to cultivate this deep knowing in our waking lives. Oftentimes this comes through experiencing a state of stillness, or space.

To create space is a practice that is essential in our times. We do this to enable our own true nature, our own stillness, and peace, to flow into life. This is a contribution that women can make to our collective consciousness. A friend of mine shared how she was extremely busy with her work, and felt a deep commitment to being of service. But she had a dream showing her that too much activity was replacing the joy she had once experienced in her work.

————

DREAM

I was told that I have become so muscular that there is no space inside me for my Self.

LIKE WAVES AT THE OCEAN, there is a pause as one wave goes out before the next wave comes in. This pause is also in our breath, as we breathe in and then out, or in nature, when we stop talking and are drawn into silence. The silence, or stillness, has something to say to us that we do not yet know.

ONE WOMAN SPOKE of a recurring dream that greatly disturbed her because she had no context in which to understand it.

> *I am in a clear, green river, resting in it, flowing along in its currents.*

The dreamer commented, "I keep having this dream. Is there something wrong with me? I've never spoken of this dream to anyone else."

If the dreamer can acknowledge that the green stream isn't outside herself, but is her divine nature, then she will be able to live in a wholly different way. Deeply conditioned to believe that the sacred could not be within her, it was difficult for her to trust this dream. Yet she was reassured that she was doing nothing 'wrong' by having such a dream, and was willing to allow herself this quality of peace, which the river evoked for her. All of us have an ancient memory of this peace, or stillness, which is why we long for it. But it takes many forms.

――――

DREAM

I dream of ancient blue tiles that also look completely modern, up-to-date. These blue tiles with desert colors evoke the longing of the heart to anyone who sees them.

THIS DREAM ALSO REFLECTS the collective longing for our essential nature, for peace. Often we have these dreams at a time when it's urgent that we be called back to the foundation of our life.

――――

DREAM

I am told to pay attention to the space between the petals of a flower.

There is a need for a quiet time each day, as distinct from gathering with others. It provides a space inside oneself. We sit still, aware of this inner space. Sometimes life will pull us into this depth. A few days after my father died, I went camping with my family. I rose early one morning to sit by the river. As I closed my eyes and listened to its rushing waters, I was drawn into a profound place of stillness and peace, while still able to hear the river. Out of this silence, I saw—as if in a dream, but I was not dreaming—the word *centerpoint*. This inner place is where we can open to the deeper meaning of our lives.

Learning the ways of *being* does not mean disengaging from life. Rather, it allows us to participate actively in a dance with life. Most importantly, you can feel the strength that comes from this orientation towards our sacred center. You can feel it in your body, like breathing fresh air, for the light of the soul is in our cells. The soul is not accessible when we are too full—of ideas, of fear, of anxieties.

DREAM

Someone tells me, "When a woman has anxiety at night, it's because she forgets that she rests in God."

PROTECTING THE STILLNESS

The nature of space or stillness is receptive. Space is the feminine, receiving aspect that allows our essential nature to come forward. It is a requirement for anything new to be born. But there is a danger posed by our patriarchal culture, which conditions women to emphasize the masculine way of *doing* and to deny their own spacious nature. When a woman comes to know the wonder and beauty of this inner feminine essence, however, her masculine energy can be rightfully applied to help hold and live this essence in her outer life.

I was reminded of the need to return to this essence when I was preparing a large forum, bringing together women from different spiritual traditions to speak about their lives. Utterly exhausted with preparations the day before the event, I went outside and lay face down on the ground, entering a deep state of sleep. In startlingly clear imagery, words came forward, one at a time, and then disappeared:

Feminine Spirit. Healing. Nourishment. Peace.

I woke up in wonder, my fatigue gone. Somehow the words themselves brought me the stillness I needed.

We may know the feminine in the cells of our body, in the longing in our heart, in a dream, but to live it requires an instinctual power that guards against our thoughts or emotions that can so easily interfere with the stillness. In a dream, this instinctual power might come as the image of the raw meat that a bobcat must eat in order to remain wild and not domesticated, or in the image of an animal, such as a bear. For each woman it will be different.

DREAM

A bear is at our front door. My husband is afraid, but I say, no, don't be afraid. I open the door and bow respectfully before the bear, and because I honored him, he will not hurt us.

WHEN WE ARE GIVEN such a dream, we can be sure that it is a gift, for it shows us the sacredness of life that we know in our depths. It is our responsibility to care for a new awareness, and to accept the power of this feminine way of being.

DREAM

A teacher shows me the feeling of stillness,
which I experience in myself. Then I lose it by
worrying about things, or by being too busy and
overwhelmed by life. He tells me that what's
needed is to be a warrior to protect the stillness.
He hands me a sword.

THE SWORD REPRESENTS the discrimination and focus needed by a woman. Otherwise she can become thrown off balance by powerful emotions or negative thoughts. She must use this sword to help her catch her doubts before they begin to cause trouble; the doubts, the fears—how easily they slip in, unnoticed until they are full-blown!

In my own dreams, doubts often appear in the symbol of ants, which show me when I need to look at what my thought patterns have been. One night, when I had to take care of a stressful outer situation, the usual ants of doubt in my dreams turned into termites. I knew that I would have to wield the sword of discernment. I had to stop thinking the thoughts that were eroding my connection to the stillness, and I needed the sword to reclaim the trust I had lost. Only then could the joy that is deep inside of life return.

PART FOUR

DREAMS:
MESSENGERS OF WISDOM

LISTENING

The ancients told of dreams from another dimension. These dreams gave prophecies, guidance and inspiration. Originally for every religion, and especially in indigenous cultures where religion and culture are intertwined, dreams and visions continue to be of utmost value.

> *For God speaketh once, yea twice, yet man*
> *perceiveth it not. In a dream, in a vision of the*
> *night, when deep sleep falleth upon men, in*
> *slumberings upon the bed; then He opened the*
> *ears of men, and sealeth their instructions.*
> —*Job 53:14–16*

Now we are at such a time, where we need to open our 'ears' to our dreams. Not as fantasy or illusion, but as a source that can inspire our imagination in its deepest and most sacred sense. Just as Martin Luther King entrusted the words "I have a dream" to a newly awakening culture, so too must we listen and respond with the same mature authority.

There are many possibilities we now hold for the future. As women become conscious of life as it changes around us, we can ask for guidance and listen to dreams. We can also learn to listen to life itself, by adapting to and focusing our attention on the new that is emerging, instead of spiraling backwards into despair or hopelessness. Some describe this practice of holding life lightly, with consciousness, as an attitude of oneness. For what are we listening to, but all of life!

A dream can tell of mud and rain, but many times, at the end of the mud and rain is a blade of grass, or even a rainbow. We can choose what daily practice to devote our energy to: the mud, or the blades of grass.

Having had such a dream, I chose to place my attention on the fresh blades of grass by holding an awareness of them in my heart. Why fresh grass? Because green grass is a symbol of life, newness, the feminine, of what grows from the earth.

In a time of great unknowing, I believed I had to give up my nonprofit women's work, but it returned in a dream. The dream showed me its value, and I knew that I could not walk away from it. If it weren't for this dream, I might have convinced myself that I wasn't worthy of this work.

DREAM

I am walking on a dusty dirt road into town,
carrying a rolled carpet on my shoulders. I am
going to give it away. It's a wool carpet from
China that I used for years in my workshops. But
I love this carpet. I don't have to sell it. I woke up
the next morning with the thought that when we
give something away, it returns to us in a new way.

NOURISHMENT

I was in North Carolina where I had been interviewed earlier by the local Asheville newspaper. That evening, in a small yoga studio in downtown Asheville, at least sixty men and women came to hear my talk about how dreamwork guides us in our soul's journey. I started to give the talk but after a few minutes I stopped. The room was full of dreams that people wanted to tell.

I asked if anyone had a dream they wanted to share, and then, one after another, people told their dreams. One man, a construction worker, told a mystical dream that he had never told anyone before. In his dream, he was in a boat in the ocean when a light came and lifted him out of the water. He heard melodies that filled him with joy. The next morning, he found that he could whistle the music that he heard in his heart. He had always wanted to whistle but could never do so.

What wonder filled the room as these dreams were spoken aloud and received. No one asked for interpretation. They just wanted to share them, to have them validated and acknowledged. It was as if the dreams simply needed to be welcomed into this world. This is the degree to which we have excluded the magic of the inner world.

As you read these dreams, allow them to speak to the place within you where your own wisdom resides. A dream nourishes the soul. We need this nourishment, as a tree needs water, as a seed needs the fertile earth to grow.

DREAMS OF

WOMEN AND THE EARTH

I am standing at the edge of a valley. There are people all along the rim watching, and as I come to the edge and look down, I see Her. An old Native woman with very wrinkled hands, wrinkled face, looks up and sees me. I lean to the person beside me and ask, "Who is that?" She says, "Don't you know? That's Grandmother Earth." As I watch, she bends down again and slowly begins sweeping away what looks like the foundation of a building. The person leans over and says to me, "She's taking care of the foundations of the world."

She holds us (many children) and rocks us slowly, then lifts up her head and begins a keening wail. The sound fills my ears, my being, my mind, and draws me into her.... As I wake up, for the first time I know the feeling of Love.

—CANADIAN ACTRESS, after years of
working on healing childhood abuse

I am walking by a forest grove, and ask Nature if there is anything I need to know. This is how I understand Nature's response: "Women want to know how best to heal the earth. They feel overwhelmed by all that is occurring now—the outward signs of how I am changing. They want to do something big, when it takes so little. All that I need is for the women to notice ... To see me...To take a moment to stop and be with me. Just pay attention to me, notice I am here. Just that, heals. It may not seem that looking with awareness at this plant, that bird, the ground beneath your feet, creates healing. And it may not look like something right here needs to be healed. But just a woman's looking, seeing me, just the touch of her hand, just her feet walking upon me is an act of healing. The energy is taken in, absorbed—and sent through me to where it's needed most."

—MARKETING CONSULTANT, California

I see an aboriginal man coming towards me out of the darkness. He says, "It is time for the women to care for the earth." He then recedes back into the darkness.

—SOCIAL WORKER FROM AUSTRALIA
(a few days after 9/11)

I am standing on the ground, and look down and see that my legs from the knees down are inside the earth. I look more closely and see that my legs have become roots that interconnect with the roots just inside the surface of the earth, all around the world. These interconnecting roots are feminine and belong to all women, but there are areas not lit up, still in darkness. I understand that these areas are where women still do not value themselves and each other.

—CLINICAL PSYCHOLOGIST with Pakistani
and British heritage, England

I wake up hearing these words from a
dream: A song to the earth of joy.

—A WRITER, South Carolina

I ask, "How can I help the earth?"
The answer comes: *Just love more.*

—ENGLISH TEACHER,
New Mexico

DREAMS OF

HEALING

It was right after 9/11. I am in a desert and a Native American man walks towards me with a stick. I ask him, "What can we do about this?" He hits me on the head with the stick and blood pours down me, into the cracks on the dry earth like rivulets. It flows all across the country, and wherever it touches I see that flowers grow out of it. It flows all the way to New York and right to the feet of a fireman. His face is exhausted and he is in despair, but a flower grows out of the blood that has flowed to his feet. This flower gives him hope and the blood nourishes the whole land.

—MAORI HEALER, Australia

I see a woman with no specific features who is clothed in a flowing burnt orange garment. The woman is bathed in a radiant light and cradles in her arms an ancient globe of the world from which a red heart pulsates.

—A GRANDMOTHER AND PSYCHOTHERAPIST
from the Midwest who works with women,
including spouses of returning Iraq war veterans

I see the earth from a distance far above. It is a beautiful, blue jewel in space, but on closer look I see inflamed areas where there is violence and war. And then I am shown the moon which is shining a light down onto the earth in rays, almost like sunlight, but softer. This light touches directly on the places of the earth where there is conflict and war. A voice says, "Wherever the feminine touches, there is healing."

—MY OWN DREAM, after I first
began to work with women

A seven-year-old girl is told, "The purpose of your life is to love God." Then I am told, "Your purpose is to cut rocks and create beauty in the world." A core of love is placed inside of me.

—A JEWELER, California

An old female elephant is pregnant, but has a large wound on her side. She begins to go into the desert where she will give birth, but a woman tells her that she should not go with that wound on her side. The elephant speaks: "I must give birth! It doesn't matter about the wound!" And she walks, and then lays down and gives birth to new life.

—WOMAN HEALING FROM TRAUMA, Germany

An older man, bearded and dressed in robes, greets me and welcomes me into a circle of people. He gently frames my face in his hands and I close my eyes. He pours olive oil from a small blue clay jar over my third eye. I remember a sense of vast space and very bright light behind my eyelids. I feel so loved. I realize that every particle of my being, both physical and spirit, is being embraced, accepted, welcomed, made whole. I don't have to clean or fix any part of me ever again. I think I have a responsibility to live that.

—A MOTHER HEALING from
childhood abuse, California

DREAMS OF

ONENESS

I am walking in a forest. I see the heads of all religions in the world, and they all have different hats on. "Come," they say. But I am terrified. I run away. They become animals in the forest. I run to the closet to hide, and then I find out they are all there, inside, waiting, each of them holding a candle. "We'll wait until you're ready."

—A NURSE, Minnesota

VISION

I was sitting on my deck, a cup of coffee in my hand,
so lost in my despair that I was annoyed by a noise
that kept interrupting my crying. I said to myself,
"I wish you'd leave me alone in my misery." But as
I listened and looked up, I saw a bird sitting on my
shed, singing to me, "Please don't cry, for it hurts me
too! I want you to see the beauty that is in you and all
of creation, for we are one. So sing with me and all of
creation to heal your soul, we are one! Sing with the
birds and nature for when you hurt, they hurt with
you, for we are one. The healing of the nations is in
this song of love."

—A SCHOOLTEACHER, Georgia

I am walking in the pitch-black night of the world, like all the darkness in the world right now. As I am walking I see a beacon of light that is surprising to me. Then, as I keep walking, I see, one by one, thousands of lights stand up out of the darkness— beacons all over the world. Each one a person, holding their own portion of light in the darkness. I get the sense that each of these beacons is outshining the darkness…and is more powerful than the darkness. The lights are lighthouses or beacons for the souls on the world to gravitate to—they will be attracted, so to speak, to the light.

—A MOTHER OF FOUR CHILDREN
and founder of a catalog company, Washington

The ordinary glass that I use every day is filled
with clear water. I see this glass lifted towards me.
I understand that when I drink from it, the glass
then tilts and pours into the collective.

—AUTHOR'S DREAM

I wake up from a dream in which I hear, "The problem is that people have forgotten they are one."

—BUSINESS DEVELOPMENT MANAGER
for on-line news delivery service, Virginia

DREAMS OF

SERVICE TO LIFE

———

I receive a phone call from my sister who has become, in real life, a Benedictine nun. She says, "Come, put the kids in the car, take your husband, and drive over here." She sounds as if it is urgent, and I'm worried that something might have happened. I ask, "Why?" And she says, "Because the Lord is here."

So I drive down there and find a huge pyramid. I walk up, spiraling around it to the top. At the top of the pyramid I see Jesus. I am so awed, as if I were a child. I want to ask a profound question, but all I say is, "You look just how I imagined you'd look."

He says, "I come by whatever visage is most familiar to you." He fills me with love, but then says he has to leave.

"Oh, take me with you," I say.

"No," he tells me, "You're not ready. There's still one thing you need to do."

—A LIBRARIAN FROM MINNESOTA
who recalls this dream from 15 years back

A voice says, "You are a piece of a hammer, blown by the wind, blown by the wind." I feel so honored. Just to be part of a tool that can be used when needed, and taken by the wind where life needs me to go. And whenever I think of it I laugh because a hammer doesn't have any emotions or troubles or need to know anything. It just is!! It is solid, it is here, it does its job, as simple as that. What could be more simple and direct than a hammer?

—COLLEGE STUDENT, Minnesota

I am walking down Main Street, when I know I have to find a drink of water. I go to a nearby park and see that there is a hole in the ground and clear water rises out of it. I realize that the water downstream becomes more polluted the further it is from this source. I have to drink as close to the source as possible.

—A MOTHER who is an artist
and hairdresser, California

I see a huge hotel swimming pool, several city blocks long. It is filled with crystal clear warm water, and I rest deeply in it. But when I leave the pool to take care of some business and return, the pool is empty! A manager says, "If women don't use it, we drain it." I wake up with a sense of urgency that women need to come together so that this water can nourish life.

—AUTHOR'S DREAM

I am at the home where I was born and grew up. It is a stone house that overlooks a canyon, near the ocean. I am standing at the house when I see the bow of a ship so huge that I can't see the end of it. It comes through a narrow valley, with only millimeters to spare on either side. The sky is filled with light, like a sunset or sunrise. The boat is on the same level as the house. I don't have to go up or down—I just walk onto the boat. I am alone and it is silent. The boat isn't scratched, and the house isn't damaged. It is amazing.

I leave the ship and know that the ship is leaving. The pilot, a woman, will steer it safely out to sea. I know it will go where it needs to go. This ship fills my heart. I recognize this ship. I claim it. I know that now I can serve.

—A DRESSMAKER AND DESIGNER born in Korea
who had this dream after the death of her husband.

I am standing in a room the size of a bedroom. It has no windows or doors, but is very expansive. I don't feel closed in at all. In the center of the room taking all the space is a sphere, which I feel is the earth. The sphere is a web of interconnecting lights, and I can see the lines connecting them. Not all of the lights are lit. I'm standing before this and I understand that it is my responsibility to tend and nurture the lights. I can find these lights at Home Depot!

—BANK MANAGER, Chicago

I am in a dressing room, preparing to be on the "American Idol" TV show. I stay in that room selecting a dress, selecting a song, and waiting for someone in charge to direct me as to what to do next. (I decide that I will sing Mariah Carey's "Hero" which has great lyrics about inner strength). Hour after hour, I expect that someone will come, but no one ever comes to tell me that it is time for me to sing. I suddenly realize I have missed a great opportunity.

—SOFTWARE PROGRAMMER,
Baton Rouge, Louisiana

A woman tells me, "You can no longer remain silent. You can no longer bow your head in silence. You must hold your head high and speak from the deepest part of yourself. Even in front of the king."

—AUTHOR'S DREAM

DREAMS OF
CONNECTION TO ESSENCE

———

I am with a faceless man who is standing close
to me. He says, "You have loved me since before
time. I see a crying in you." When I wake up I
feel an intimacy I have never known before.
I didn't know that I had this love inside of me.

—FROM A MOTHER AND BUSINESS OWNER,
Colorado

I meet a man who is holding my hand. He says to me, "I don't even know if I believe in the ineffable. My brain certainly doesn't. But if you look into my eyes, you will feel it." I then look into his eyes where I see a vast ocean, and am filled with peace.

—AN ADMINISTRATOR in Oregon

My whole body seems to become the universe and there are fibers of light, interconnecting everything with everything else, like the delicate threads of a dandelion seed.

—MINISTER and children's
book author, England

A woman gives me a necklace. It's gold with a small green stone that rests in the hollow of my throat. Someone whispers my name to her. This name has an ancient sound. When I wake up I can't remember the name, only its sacred quality.

—A BUSINESS OWNER in Georgia

I was told that each woman has a light inside, whether she knows it or not. This is the light that she sees by, knows by, and *is*. This light belongs to the Creator. This light also belongs to the whole.

—A MOTHER who works as an office administrator, Nebraska. "It is when I am in despair that a dream comes to show me what I need to know about my life, even when I don't want to know it."

THE LANTERN OF OUR LIVES

This book is an invitation to respect and hold the dreams that are given to us, and to recognize them as gifts from beyond. Dreams may not make our lives easier, but they can help us to live more mindfully, aligned with the soul.

No one has all the solutions to the global problems that we have inherited, but one way to find solutions is to become conscious of how we live our lives. Each of us has a part to play and a gift to share. By relating to dreams, we each can learn how we resonate with the world, and bring forth this understanding into our lives.

A friend from England wrote to me about how women in the eighth century would stand along the craggy southern coast, holding lanterns for the fisherman at sea. Her story caught my attention, drawing me into the image of women getting up in the dark, leaving their homes to hold a light with other women.

How many times do women get up in the dark, whether to attend to a child, or to pray for someone close to them? We are now being asked to come forward, to be awake to life in a different way. May we carry the lantern of our lives into the world.

ACKNOWLEDGMENTS

I AM DEEPLY GRATEFUL TO THE WOMEN who have generously shared their dreams and visions for this book. I give special thanks and appreciation to Zakira Beasley, Karen Jurgens, Ginny Matthews, Lynda Terry, and Paulette Fox, with whom I have led retreats over the past few years. They are part of a community of women working together to bring forth feminine spiritual values in their lives and in our culture. I would also like to thank Christina O'Reilly, whose encouragement for this book was invaluable. Finally, I would like to acknowledge the contribution of Diana Badger whose editing of this book was done with great attention and care.

PERMISSIONS

With appreciation for the quotation of Hazrat Inayat Khan from an unknown source. For further information about Hazrat Inayat Khan, contact www.sufiorder.org

For permission to use copyrighted material, the author gratefully wishes to acknowledge: Shirley Mast at the Mennonite Central Committee, for permission to quote a dream from the video "After Sexual Abuse," featuring Vicki Dyck.

ABOUT THE AUTHOR

ANNE SCOTT, founder of DreamWeather Foundation, leads workshops and retreats for women in diverse communities and organizations around the country. The focus of her work is restoring the link between feminine wisdom and social change, and on the healing nature of dreams. Anne was a speaker at the United Nations Peace Initiative in Geneva, Switzerland, and at a global conference in Jaipur, India: *Making Way for the Feminine for the Benefit of the World Community*, in 2008. She has trained in spiritual dreamwork in the Naqshbandi Sufi Path for 19 years. Anne is the author of *Serving Fire: Food for Thought, Body and Soul* and *The Laughing Baby*, and lives with her husband in northern California.

You can reach Anne at:

DreamWeather Foundation

P.O. Box 2002

Sebastopol, CA 95473

www.dreamweather.org

CPSIA information can be obtained at www.ICGtesting.com
Printed in the USA
LVOW091728270212

270651LV00011B/172/P

9 780981 863610